MW01640000

Tim Spacum MERRY CHRISTMAS 2014

THE BUTTERFLY EFFECT

HOW YOUR LIFE MATTERS

Dedicated to Doug and Julie Cassens, Mike and Lynn Jakubik, and Todd and Brenda Rainsberger. You are such an important part of our lives, yet it is through this amazing principle that we even met!

AUTHOR'S NOTE

Not long ago, I finally told the story of when, at the age of twenty-three, homeless and scared, I was given guidance in a most unusual fashion by an old man named Jones. I remember completing the manuscript for *The Noticer* and being somewhat troubled by the fact that there were so many incredible moments with Jones that I hadn't been able to include. After all, he'd done nothing less than change absolutely *everything* about my life and future. I needn't have worried. The conversation I am about to reveal deserved a book of its own anyway...

"With a little perspective," Jones said one day,
"you can live *a life of permanent purpose.*"

When I asked what he meant, the old man answered with a question. "Do you sometimes find yourself unconsciously judging your actions by level of importance?" I frowned a bit, not certain I understood. "For instance, "he continued, "the time you spend with friends is important, but the time you spend with family, is *more* important. You might rank an hour fishing as very important, thirty minutes visiting a sick friend in the hospital much more important than the fishing, and a sixty second conversation with a convenience store clerk as not very important at all."

I nodded my understanding and he returned to his initial point. "When you *know* that everything matters—that *every move* counts as much as any other—you will begin living a life of permanent purpose. A life of permanent purpose will make you a better parent, a better spouse and a more valuable friend. Your productivity and financial success will soar to new heights while the old days of uncertainty, doubt, and depression fade into the past."

Of course, that conversation with Jones changed me. But even more, it became the guiding force that produced the kind of speaker and author I have become. You see, I understand fully that my very value as an author and speaker must ultimately be judged by the *success you achieve.* And as I consult with companies or speak to organizations and teams, I am keenly aware that much of my client's (your) ability to succeed beyond imagination depends upon my ability to prove this very concept!

When a sales organization sees *proof* that casual conversations in town matter just as much as an arranged meeting with a major prospect—

When the second string right-guard sees *proof* that his every action on and off the field, whether he plays or not, is as critical to the team's successful season as everything the starting quarterback does—

When a teenager sees and understands *proof* that every choice made in leisure today will affect the choices that will be available to him in more pressing times ahead—

When one lives a life of permanent purpose, sales figures soar, team chemistry thrives and teenage decisions become wiser and more cautious. And these are just a few examples of what will happen... Simply put, when we understand that every action matters, every result of our actions immediately improves!

In these pages, I know you will find hope and direction for yourself, but I am most excited that you will now be equipped to lead others to their own life of permanent purpose! My hope for our families, our places of worship, our businesses, our nation and our world is an incredible life of permanent purpose that can be achieved when at last we understand: Every move we make and every action we take, matters not just for us, but for all of us ... *and for all time.*

Andy Andrews
Orange Beach, Alabama

How SIGNIFICANT is my life?

Do I make a difference?

When I *move* ...
when I *act* ...
when I *do something* ...

does the universe notice?

Do I REALLY matter?

In 1963,

Edward Lorenz presented a hypothesis to the New York Academy of Science. His theory, stated simply, was that:

A butterfly could flap its wings and set molecules of air in motion, which would move other molecules of air, in turn moving more molecules of air—eventually capable of starting a hurricane on the other side of the planet.

Lorenz and his ideas were literally laughed out of the conference. What he had proposed was ridiculous.

It was preposterous.
But it was fascinating!

Therefore, because of the idea's charm and intrigue, the so-called "butterfly effect" became a staple of science fiction, remaining for decades a combination of myth and legend spread only by comic books and bad movies.

So imagine the scientific community's shock and surprise when, more than thirty years after the possibility was introduced, physics professors working from colleges and universities worldwide came to the conclusion that the butterfly effect was *authentic, accurate, and viable*.

Soon after, it was accorded the status of a "law." Now known as ***The Law of Sensitive Dependence Upon Initial Conditions***, this principle has proven to be a force encompassing more than mere butterfly wings.

Science has shown the butterfly effect to
engage with the first movement of any
form of matter—including people.

that there once existed a single man
who, more than a century ago,
MADE ONE MOVE...
that still dramatically affects
how you live today?

He was a thirty-four year old schoolteacher, but on the hot, humid day of July 2, 1863, Joshua Lawrence Chamberlain was in the fight of his life.

A former professor of rhetoric from Bowdoin College in Maine, he was now a Colonel in the Union Army. Chamberlain stood at the far left edge of a group of eighty thousand men strung out in a line across fields and hills, stretching all the way to a little town called Gettysburg, Pennsylvania.

Earlier that day, a Colonel Vincent had placed Chamberlain and his men of the 20th Maine at the end of that line, saying,

***"Whatever you do,
you can't let them
come through here."***

Chamberlain couldn't withdraw and he knew it. If the Confederate Army overran them, the rebels would gain the high ground, and the Union Army would be quickly defeated. In essence, eighty thousand men would be caught from behind on a downhill charge with no protection. To win, the grey clad Confederates would have to come through Chamberlain.

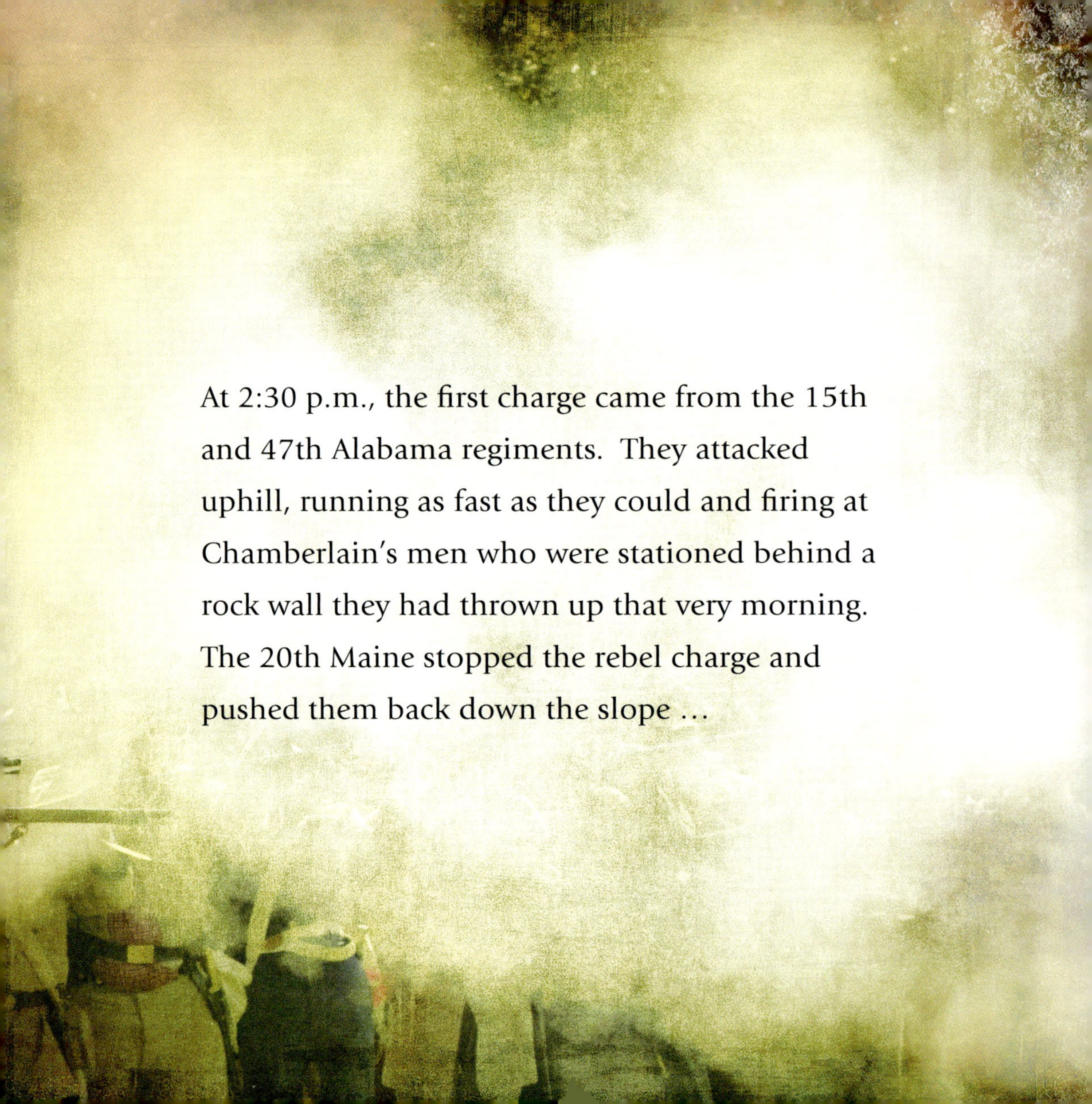

At 2:30 p.m., the first charge came from the 15th and 47th Alabama regiments. They attacked uphill, running as fast as they could and firing at Chamberlain's men who were stationed behind a rock wall they had thrown up that very morning. The 20th Maine stopped the rebel charge and pushed them back down the slope …

ONLY TO FACE A
SECOND

THEN A
THIRD
CHARGE!

On the fourth assault, Chamberlain was knocked down by a bullet that hit him dead center—in the belt buckle. Realizing that he wasn't seriously hurt, the Colonel scrambled to his feet, continuing to fight. Again, they halted the enemy's charge and again, the rebels retreated down the hill.

At that time in history, battles were fought with artillery and small arms ammunition.

THE STRUGGLES WERE

CLOSE, FACE-TO-FACE AFFAIRS.

With their fourth charge, the Confederates almost made it to the wall—a thigh high stack of flat rocks that ran almost one hundred and ten yards in length.

As they waited for the next charge, Chamberlain felt sorry for his men. He later recalled, "Their leader had no real knowledge of warfare or tactics. I was only a stubborn man and that was my greatest advantage in this fight.

I had,
deep within me,
the inability to do
NOTHING."

Chamberlain continued, "I knew I may die, but I also knew that I would not die with a bullet in my back. I would not die in retreat. I am, at least, like the apostle Paul who wrote,

'This one thing I do, I press toward the mark.'"

The attack came again. On this, the fifth charge, the 15th and 47th Alabama broke open the wall and fighting raged on both sides. Without time to reload, the men were swinging their rifles at each other and brawling with fists and knives.

Somehow,
the 20th Maine
pushed the rebels
downhill
another time.

After that fifth broken charge, Chamberlain's younger brother, Tom, appeared with Sergeant Tozier, an old, hard-nosed soldier. Tozier had a thick wad of torn shirt stuck into a hole in his shoulder where he had been wounded.

"No help from the 83rd," the Sergeant said. "They're shot to ribbons and all they can do is extend the line a bit. We're getting murdered on our flank."

"Can we extend?" Chamberlain asked.

"There's nothing to extend," Tom answered.

"More than half our men are down."

It was true. Chamberlain's command had started in Bangor, Maine, six months earlier, with a thousand men. They'd started that morning with three hundred. Now they were down to eighty.

"How are we for ammunition?" the Colonel asked.

"We've been shooting a lot," was his brother's answer.

"I know we've been shooting a lot," Chamberlain snapped.

"I want to know how we're holding out. How much ammunition do we have left?"

As Tom ran to check, a twelve-year-old lookout had climbed a tree. He yelled,

"They're forming up again, Colonel!"

Chamberlain looked up to see the boy pointing down the hill. "They're forming up right now. And they've been reinforced.

Sir, there's a lot more of them this time."

At that moment, a messenger stumbled into their midst. Out of breath, he said, "Sir! Colonel Chamberlain, sir! Colonel Vincent is dead."

"Are you sure, soldier?"

"Yes, sir," he gasped. "He was shot right at the first of the fight. They were firmed up by Weeds Brigade, but now Weeds is dead. They moved Hazlett's Battery up top. Hazlett's dead, too."

Chamberlain's brother came running back.

"Joshua," he said,

"WE'RE OUT!

One ... two rounds per man at the most.

Some of the men don't have anything at all!"

Chamberlain turned to a thin man standing on his right. It was First Sergeant Ellis Spear. "Spear," he ordered, "tell the boys to take the ammunition from the wounded and the dead."

"We did that last time, sir," Spear replied. "Maybe we should think about pulling out."

Chamberlain responded grimly, "We will not be pulling out, Sergeant. Carry out my orders please."

"Colonel!" Sergeant Tozier spoke up. "We won't hold them again, sir. You know we won't!"

"JOSHUA!"
IT WAS HIS BROTHER.
"HERE THEY COME!
HERE THEY COME!"

Chamberlain stepped to the top of the wall in full view, crossing his arms and staring down at the advancing enemy.

The 15th and 47th Alabama with their pale, yellow-gray uniforms, now reinforced by a Texas regiment, moved up the hill as their high pitched shriek—the rebel yell—coursed up toward Chamberlain and his men. Sergeant Spear was standing at the Colonel's feet. Sergeant Tozier, Chamberlain's brother Tom, and Lieutenant Melcher, the flag bearer, were huddled below. "Joshua!" his brother said. "Do something!

GIVE AN ORDER!"

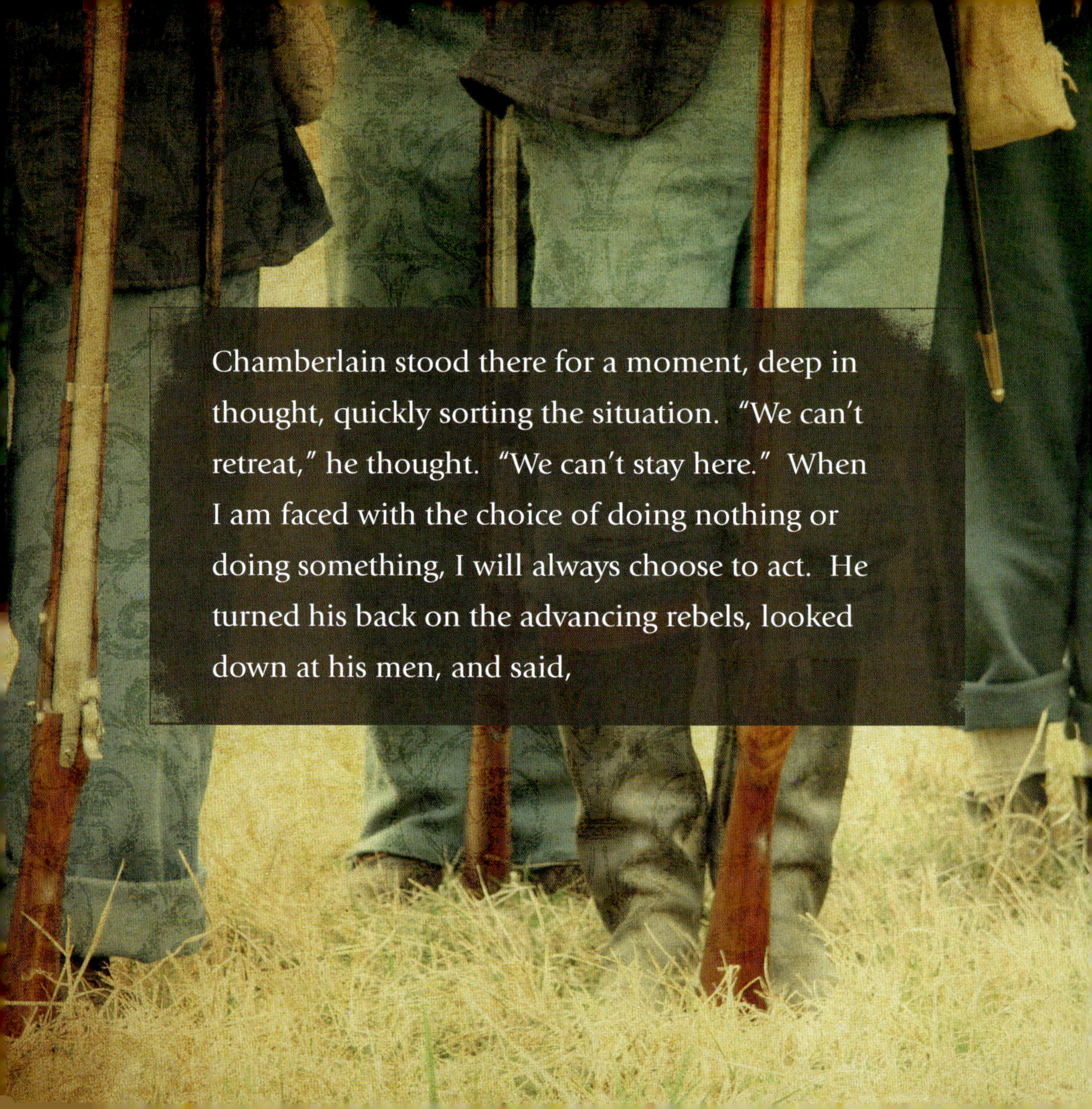

Chamberlain stood there for a moment, deep in thought, quickly sorting the situation. "We can't retreat," he thought. "We can't stay here." When I am faced with the choice of doing nothing or doing something, I will always choose to act. He turned his back on the advancing rebels, looked down at his men, and said,

"FIX BAYONETS!"

At first, no one moved. They just stared at him with their mouths open.

"FIX YOUR BAYONETS NOW!"

he commanded again.

"EXECUTE A GREAT RIGHT WHEEL OF THE ENTIRE REGIMENT.

Swing the left first. Do it now!"

Lieutenant Melcher spoke first, confused. "Sir," he asked, "What is a great right wheel?" But the Colonel had already jumped from the wall and was moving to the next group of men. Sergeant Tozier answered the question.

"HE MEANS TO CHARGE, SON.

A GREAT RIGHT WHEEL IS AN ALL-OUT CHARGE."

Then, turning, the Colonel pointed his sword directly downhill. Facing overwhelming odds, Chamberlain slashed his blade through the air and with a power born of courage and fear, the schoolteacher from Maine roared,

"CHARGE!
CHARGE!
CHARGE!"

to his men.

The remaining eighty fighting men lifted their voices to match that of their leader. "Charge! Charge!" they cried tumbling over the wall into a history about which most people in our country have never heard.

For when the Confederate troops saw Chamberlain, the leader of the opposition, mount the wall they immediately stopped, unsure as to what was happening. And when the Colonel pointed his sword toward them and commanded his men to charge, they turned and ran. Many threw down their loaded weapons.

The rebels were certain that these were not the same soldiers they had been facing. Surely these men have been reinforced, they thought. A beaten regiment would not charge. In less than five minutes, Chamberlain had his sword on the collarbone of a Confederate captain.

"You, sir, are my prisoner," he stated.

The man turned around a fully loaded Navy Colt revolver and offered it to Chamberlain. "Yes sir," he answered. "I am."

Within five more minutes, that ragged group of eighty men under Chamberlain's command—without any ammunition—captured over four hundred soldiers of the enemy.

It is an amazing story, isn't it? And absolutely true.

BUT HERE'S WHAT MOST PEOPLE
NEVER CONSIDER...

Historians have determined that had Chamberlain not charged that day, the rebels would have won at Gettysburg.

Further, historians tell us, had the rebels won at Gettysburg, the South would have won the war … and the war itself would have been over by the end of the summer.

Most people assume that had the South won the war, today we would exist as two countries,

THE UNION
AND THE
CONFEDERACY.

Historians however, insist that if the South had won the war, we would now live on a territorially fragmented continent much like Europe—

MUCH LIKE EUROP

North America would be divided into nine to thirteen countries.

Which means:

When Hitler swept across Europe in the 1940s, had Chamberlain not charged on that afternoon so long ago, there would not have existed a United States of America to stand in the breach.

DEUTSCHE
1024
REICH

WHEN HIROHITO SYSTEMATICALLY INVADED THE ISLANDS OF THE SOUTH PACIFIC, THERE WOULD NOT HAVE BEEN A COUNTRY

BIG
ENOUGH,

STRONG
ENOUGH,

WEALTHY
ENOUGH,

&

POPULOUS
ENOUGH,

TO FIGHT AND WIN
TWO WARS ON TWO FRONTS
AT THE SAME TIME.

The United States of America
exists as it does today
because of a single man:

One thirty-four year old schoolteacher and one move he made more than a century ago.

Don't you see?

Joshua Lawrence Chamberlain is a human example of the butterfly effect. One man who made one move whose effects still ripple through your life today.

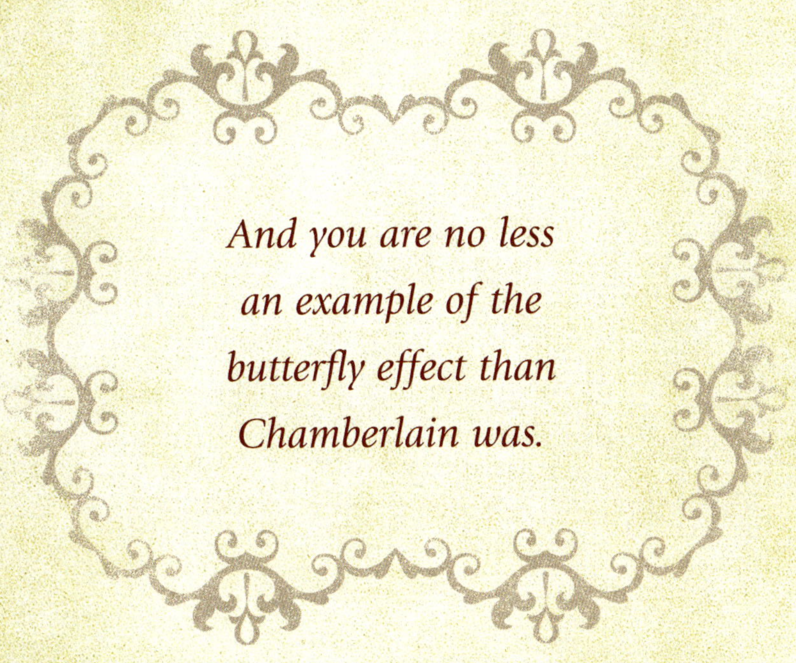

And you are no less an example of the butterfly effect than Chamberlain was.

EVERYTHING YOU DO MATTERS.

EVERY MOVE YOU MAKE,
EVERY ACTION YOU TAKE …
MATTERS.

Not just to
YOU,

or your
FAMILY,

or your
BUSINESS

or
HOMETOWN.

Everything you do matters

TO ALL OF US

FOREVER.

On Friday, April 2, 2004, *ABC News* honored a man who, at that time, was ninety-one years old.

The news program was running a regular segment called

"PERSON OF THE WEEK."

Usually, the honoree's accomplishments are listed in advance and by the time the name is announced, most folks have already guessed the identity of that week's recipient. In this instance, however, the pronouncement left many viewers puzzled.

PERSON OF THE WEEK

"And so …
our Person of the Week is …"

the anchorman finally said,

"...NORMAN
BORLAUG!"

One can only imagine the frowns.

WHO? WHO DID HE SAY?

Norman ... what was the last name? Yet, despite our unfamiliarity, Norman Borlaug is a man who is personally responsible for drastically and dramatically changing the world in which we live.

You see, in the early 1940s, Norman Borlaug hybridized high yield, disease resistant corn and wheat for arid climates.

From the dust bowl of
Western Africa to our own
desert Southwest...
from South and Central America
to the plains of Siberia ...
across Europe and Asia ...

Borlaug's specific seed product flourished and regenerated where no seed had ever thrived before.

Through the years, it has now been calculated that Norman Borlaug's work saved from famine more than two billion lives.

Actually, it was never reported, but the anchorman was misinformed. It was not Norman Borlaug who saved the two billion people, though very few caught the mistake.

IT WAS A MAN NAMED
HENRY WALLACE.

HENRY WALLACE
WAS THE
VICE PRESIDENT
OF THE
UNITED STATES
UNDER
FRANKLIN ROOSEVELT.

"Wait a minute!" you might exclaim. "I thought Harry Truman was the Vice President under Roosevelt." That is very true, but remember, Roosevelt served four terms. He had three different Vice Presidents and the second man to serve as Roosevelt's Vice President, from 1941-1945 was Henry Wallace.

Wallace was the former Secretary of Agriculture who, after his one term as Vice President, was dumped from the ticket in favor of Truman. While Wallace was Vice President, however, he used the power of that office to create a station in Mexico whose sole purpose was to hybridize corn and wheat for arid climates.

And he hired a young man named Norman Borlaug to run it.

So Norman Borlaug won the Nobel Prize. And Norman Borlaug was awarded the Presidential Medal of Freedom. But considering the connection ... it was really Henry Wallace that saved the two billion people!

SVERIGES RIKSBANK TILL ALFRED NOBELS MINNE

Or was it George Washington Carver? You remember Carver, don't you?

The peanut...?

But here's something that very few people know ... When Carver was nineteen years old and a student at Iowa State University, he had a dairy sciences professor who, on Saturday and Sunday afternoons, would allow his six-year-old boy to go on "botanical expeditions" with the brilliant student.

It was George Washington Carver who took that boy and instilled in him a love for plants and a vision for what they could do for humanity. It was George Washington Carver who pointed six-year-old Henry Wallace's life in a specific direction—long before he ever became Vice President of the United States.

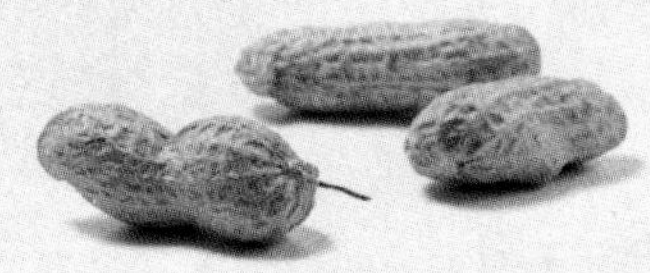

It is amazing to contemplate, isn't it? George Washington Carver flapping his butterfly wings with the peanut ...

THERE ARE CURRENTLY 266 THINGS HE DEVELOPED FROM THE PEANUT THAT WE STILL USE TODAY.

He flapped his wings with the sweet potato ...

THERE ARE 88 THINGS CARVER ORIGINATED FROM THE SWEET POTATO THAT WE STILL USE TODAY.

And while no one was even looking, George Washington Carver flapped his wings a couple of times with a six-year-old boy …

AND JUST HAPPENED TO SAVE THE LIVES
OF MORE THAN

TWO BILLION PEOPLE...

(and counting)

So maybe it should have been
George Washington Carver—
Person of the Week!

Or the farmer from
Diamond, Missouri?

Moses and his wife Susan lived in a slave state, but they didn't believe in slavery. This was a problem for psychopaths like Quantrill's Raiders who terrorized the area by destroying property, burning and killing.

And sure enough, one cold January night, Quantrill's Raiders rode through Moses and Susan's farm. The outlaws burned the barn, shot several people, and dragged off a woman named Mary Washington who refused to let go of her infant son, George.

Mary Washington was Susan's best friend and with his wife distraught, Moses quickly sent word out through neighbors and towns and two days later managed to secure a meeting with the bandits.

On a black horse, Moses rode several hours north to a crossroads in Kansas. There, at the appointed time, in the middle of the night, he met four of Quantrill's Raiders. They were on horseback, carrying torches, and flour sacks tied over their heads with holes cut out for their eyes. There, Moses traded the only horse he had left on his farm for what they threw him in a dirty burlap bag.

As they thundered off on their horses, Moses fell to his knees and there, alone on that dark winter night, the farmer pulled from the bag a cold … naked … almost dead … baby boy.

Quickly, he jerked open his coat and his shirts and placed the child next to his skin. Covering him then with his own clothes and relying on the warmth from his own body, the man turned ... and walked that baby out.

Moses walked through the night and into the next morning to get the child to safety. He sang to the child and told him he would care for him. He promised the boy he would educate him to honor his mother, whom they knew was already dead.

That was the night that the farmer gave that baby his name. And that is how Moses and Susan Carver came to raise that little baby,

GEORGE WASHINGTON.

So when you think about it,
maybe it was the farmer from
Diamond, Missouri who saved
the two billion people.

UNLESS...

Is there an ending to this story?

Exactly who was it that saved the two billion lives? Is there a specific person to whom we could point? How far back would we have to go? How many lives would we need to examine in order to determine who it really was whose action saved two billion people … a number that continues to increase every minute?

And how far *forward* would we need to go in *your life* to show the difference you make?

There are generations yet unborn whose very lives will be shifted and shaped by the moves you make and the actions you take today. And tomorrow. And the next day. And the next.

Every single thing you do **matters.**

You have been created as one of a kind.

On the planet Earth, there has never been one like you … and there never will be again.

Your spirit, your thoughts and feelings, your ability to reason and act all exist in no one else.

The rarities that make you special are no mere accident or quirk of fate.

YOU HAVE BEEN CREATED
IN ORDER THAT YOU MIGHT
MAKE A DIFFERENCE.

YOU HAVE WITHIN YOU
THE POWER TO CHANGE
THE WORLD.

Know that your actions cannot be

HOARDED,

SAVED FOR LATER,

OR USED SELECTIVELY.

By your hand, millions—billions—of
lives will be altered, caught up in a
chain of events begun by you this day.

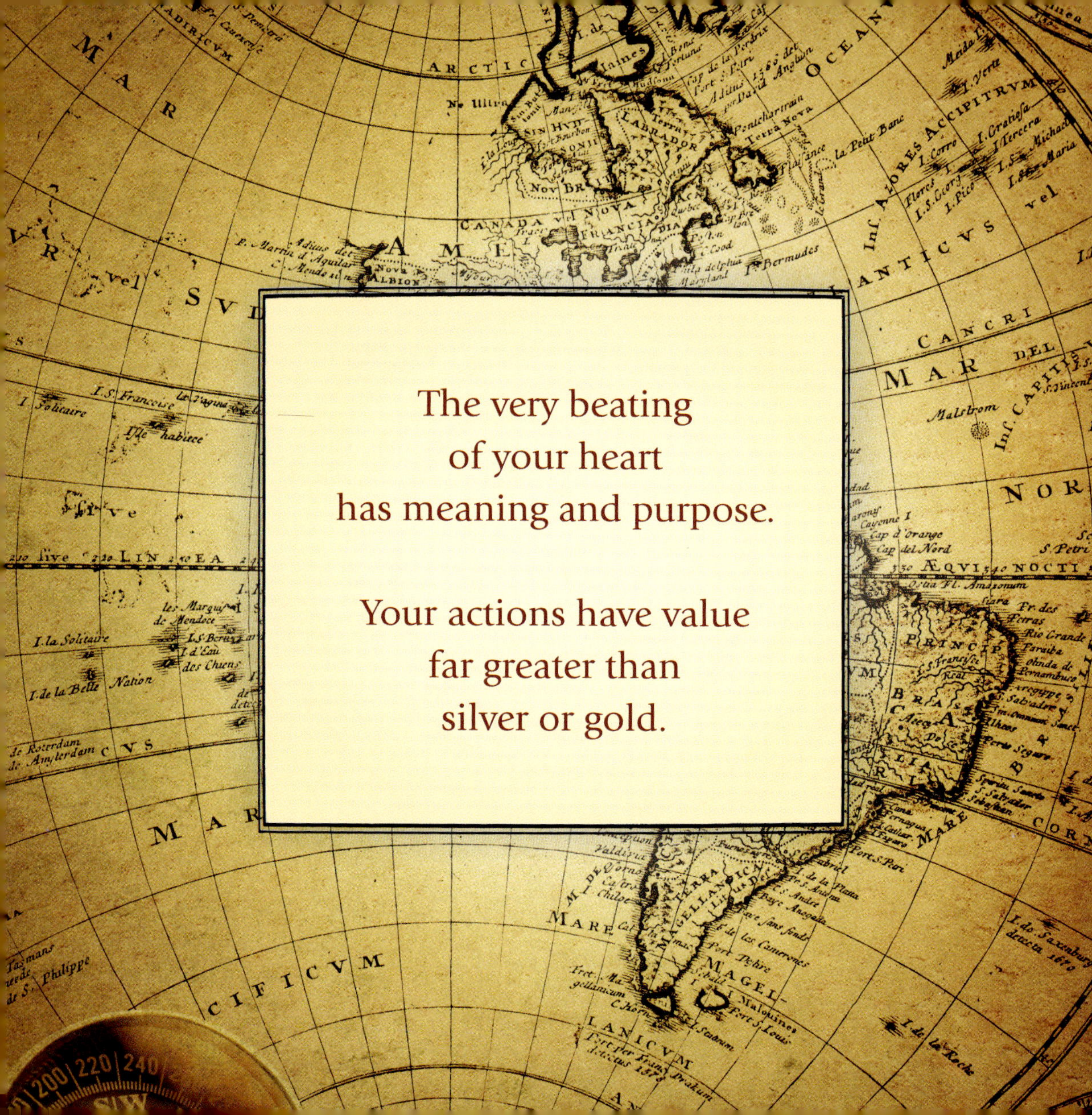

The very beating
of your heart
has meaning and purpose.

Your actions have value
far greater than
silver or gold.

Your life …
And what you do with it today …

MATTERS FOREVER.

ANDY ANDREWS, hailed by a *New York Times* writer as someone who has quietly become "one of the most influential people in America," is a best-selling novelist and in-demand corporate speaker for the world's largest organizations. He has spoken at the request of four different U.S. Presidents and at military bases worldwide. Andy is *The New York Times* Bestselling author of *The Traveler's Gift, The Lost Choice, Island of Saints, The Noticer,* and *Return to Sawyerton Springs*. He lives in Orange Beach, Alabama, with his wife, Polly, and their two sons.

To book Andy for corporate events, call

(800) 726-ANDY (2639)

Learn more at

ANDYANDREWS.com

Published by SimpleTruths, LLC
1952 McDowell Road, Suite 300
Naperville, Illinois 60563
800-900-3427
www.simpletruths.com

Design and production: Jared McDaniel, Studio430.com

All photos provided by Shutterstock.com

Printed and bound in the United States of America

ISBN 978-1-60810-028-6

07 WOZ 12